Ocean to Ocean

N. Luna

BookLeaf
Publishing

India | USA | UK

Presentation by *BookLeaf Publishing*

Web: www.bookleafpub.com

E-mail: info@bookleafpub.com

ISBN: 9789363303362

First edition 2024

Santiago

Saray

Samuel

Jhulian

Eileen

Yoshua

Alexa

ACKNOWLEDGEMENT

To Lestat who endured all this traveling like a
champ

March 3rd, 2023
Ithaca, NY

1

Driving through a snowstorm in the dark of
night
the light beams of the car let you see the space
occupied by snowflakes going in a single
direction
Reminding us that the void isn't empty
as the air is also a substance that we move
through freely
Unlike the snow, we are attached to the ground
by gravity, but what if we weren't?
What if we are also floating, occupying space,
moving in a direction,

Snowing

Nothing grows in winter, but nothing dies either.
The trees are just resting, surviving until the next
bloom.

April 14, 2023
Brooklyn, NY

Levels of healing:

First, you exist in your body: acknowledgment
Second, you make sure it is habitable: survival
Then, you make sure that all the small parts
work: health care
Lastly, you decorate: expression

May 20, 2023
Egg Harbor, NJ

First time camping alone.
Things I forgot to pack:
Melatonin
Paper towels
Hand broom
Lavender spray
Wipes
Dish soap
More plastic bags
Aluminum foil
Nail clippers
Newspapers
Teeth cup
Hammock tarp
Stakes

May 20, 2023
Egg Harbor, NJ

Saturday 5:29 pm
I like the verb: to vibe
I want to vibe more
Vibing, according to me, means to chill at the
frequency of the universe
Some people achieve this by meditating
Breathwork
Sound baths
Music
For me,
It happens when I am in the ecosystem,
Connected to the elements
Aware of the air in the space I occupy
I am welcomed
I exist
I just am
I am vibing

June 18, 2023
Wildwood State Park, NY

Do not cook potatoes on an open fire for 20
minutes
Wasted three potatoes and two carrots
The sound is the ocean
But it does not feel as vast
When we got to the end,
Of this very long island
We saw the whole sea
An open ocean
The most fulfilling void
Everything was blue
Waves merging into clouds
The universe is all there is
One gigantic thing much larger than the ocean

June 19, 2023
Wildwood State Park, NY

How beautiful it is to be wanted
I am glad you are here
That you are here for you
Wanted and loved by you

June 20, 2023
Wildwood State Park, NY

To go where I need to go
    (the bottom of the ocean where Yemaya is
         Olokun)
I have to swim inward
Into the darkness of myself
My grief, my trauma, my evil
I don't know if I can hold my breath for that
long
I've got asthma

 I am grateful for the words of women who came
                    before me

July 6, 2023
Philadelphia, PA

Sola
Asi estoy
Asi me siento
Nunca de primer lugar
Desde 1999

August 19, 2023
Croton Point Park

I can live like this
I am content with the work if it leads here
To the sounds of the woods
To the concerts of crickets
Crackling fire
Parties far away
A river running in either direction
Dogs barking
Critters scrambling in the bushes
And I, singing to the moon
I can almost hear the stars
Is it a love story if it does not have an ending?
I love myself and I brought myself here
That is love.

September 10, 2023

Port Aransas Beach, TX

How is it that I drove to Texas and then came to
the beach?
This was such a faraway dream
Yet here I am, in the Gulf of Mexico
Only a few people at the beach.
So incredibly blue
I am here to swim
I got a snorkel kit
I cannot stay out too long today
So I am going to make these few moments count
My body is at peace, my heart is at peace

September 15, 2023
Aransas Pass, TX

I live on the road now I guess
Sometimes I stop
I get out of the car and I step into the ocean.
They call it a bay
The sunset has a lot more orange here
I found a pelican bone

September 18, 2023
Magnolia beach, TX

I say never in my wildest dreams
I imagined myself here
But that cannot be true
I did dream this
Then planned it
Then executed it
Now I am at this beach that has gazebos where I
can hang my hammock
There is grass growing and wildflowers
The pictures will be amazing
I was able to read 68 pages in one sitting last
night
That's a real feature when your brain has
depression
I am a short-term person
I can only look forward to the immediate future
And traveling around is all I see now.

October 2, 2023
Placitas, NM

*"I am like this. I was born like this and I will die like
this, with all of my defects I already know it.
I am like this, and I know very well I will never
change and I accept my destiny as is."*
-Song by Jose Jose 1987

That was the line I was looking for
"I accept my destiny as is"
Everything is going okay
I was born to wander
Although I have too much stuff and I cannot
continue indefinitely.
But back to the destiny part:
I feel I spent too much time fighting my solitude
Now that I enjoy it, everything seems so trivial
I have not been in love in so long,
I do not even miss it
Alone with my music is how I am happy
I am in the mountains
In a house of adobe
I love it all
So far so good
10/10 and there will be more

October 10, 2023, Albuquerque, NM

"You are going to end up alone"
People say to me as a threat
But I don't understand why
I am alone
I have been alone
And I am fine
Well, the planet is dying
But I go on
I do not understand the whole pairing up two by
two thing

The other people in your life are "just friends"
What do you mean, "JUST" friends?
Is there anything greater than a friend?

I do not regret anything about that fight with
those friends all those many months ago.
I understand I was not eloquent
I did not use the acceptable words
But I spoke the truth and truth does not fight
anyone
Those friends can deny what happened
But I was there
I am one and they are many so I was bound to
lose
In the end, I think wanting your friends to listen
is not too much to ask
Wanting to talk to your friends is not too much
to ask
Wanting to see them, be present, be included,
this is normal

But no.
I am no one's family and no one's wife
I will always be "Just a friend"

November 23, 2023
Half-moon Bay, CA

Here I am at the ocean shore
Pulled the queen of cups
This ocean life is for me
I don't know why some dreams come true
And others don't
But I am glad I got this one

January 14, 2024
Salento, Quindio

Writing in this little notebook with seven
stitches in my finger hurts
but I am so happy to be here
to see these mountains
to climb these hills
to experience the sunset
I am not sure why it took me so long to travel
but this is my time
this is my best moment
in the depths of my soul I will plant flowers and
stars
I will grow birds and turtles

my heart will be an ecosystem of love and
support
a place for me to live and for others to find
respite
I love this day
and my brother

January 24th, 2024
Soledad, Atlantico

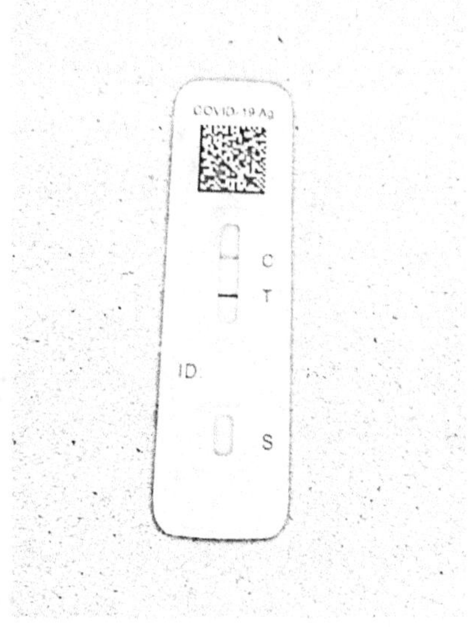

I have covid-19
It took almost 4 years to get me
I've had three vaccines
It feels like a severe nasal infection
with a massive headache and then some
I am drinking oregano, ginger, curcumin, and
Tylenol
I am fine
it is nice to have support and be taken care of
it is nice to have a family if only for 3 months
I want soup though

I have no words to express my gratitude
For everything I have and everything I am
16 people in a house with a pool
Rice and lentils
Tuna with crackers
Gossip
What a great life

Febrero 24, 2024
Barranquilla, Atlantico

Saying goodbye will never be easy
Though I have so much practice
Although I say it is not goodbye
A farewell may not be pretty
But it always leads to a welcoming
The Moon granted me this miracle in which I
had stopped believing
The river brought me smiles
The breeze gave me strength to go on
To go on doing what?
I do not know. But I go on.
It's nice to be surrounded by nieces, cousins,
friends

A wavy river
An orange moon
Strong palm trees
Corozo beer
And arequipe ice cream

March 15, 2024
Vallejo, CA

It's nice to be able to walk around your
neighborhood
There are plenty of flowers and is relatively
clean
Great sunset views over the Napa River
And the bus comes here
I can walk to the library and check out CDs like
it's 1997.
I wish it was 1997, or any other time.
It is beautiful here
There is a fancy clock
And yet I am still depressed

Haiku to Lestat

Grey splash on white fur

    yellow eyes and pointy ears

        little paws, sharp claws

www.ingramcontent.com/pod-product-compliance
Lightning Source LLC
La Vergne TN
LVHW021342200726
843509LV00014B/2632